The Stoic Teacher: Reinventing the classroom with ancient Stoic Wisdom

Alana Armstrong

Alana Armstong

The art in this book was created with assistance from DALL-E and Canva

Armstrong, Alana. The Stoic Teacher: Reinventing the Classroom with Ancient Stoic Wisdom: by Amazon, Acheson, AB/p.m. copyright 2024 ISBN: 9798336671599

"No great thing is created suddenly, any more than a bunch of grapes or a fig. If you tell me that you desire a fig, I answer you that there must be time. Let it first blossom, then bear fruit, then ripen."— **Epictetus**

Alana Armstong

Dedication: This book is dedicated to my many Cogito program students who shone like beacons of light, and understood and applied the gift of Stoicism into their lives at a young age.

Contact me for Comic book themed Stoic Superhero Teaching Materials at: thestoicteacherwisdom@gmail.com

Table of Contents

Page	Title	Topic
8	Introduction	
11	Chapter 1:	Addressing the Challenges in North American Education
15	Chapter 2:	Drawing Inspiration from Ancient Greek Stoicism
19	Chapter 3:	Building Emotional Resilience in the Educator
23	Chapter 4:	What can I do? Focusing on What's Within Your Control
28	Chapter 5:	Being Authentic through Virtue and Integrity
32	Chapter 6:	Stoic Principles for Teachers
37	Chapter 7:	Cultivating Stoic-Based Meditations for Daily Practice
41	Chapter 8:	Practical Applications of Stoicism in the Classroom

44	Chapter 9:	Winning Over Parents and Students
48	Chapter 10:	Practical Integration of Stoicism into Classroom Activities
53	Chapter 11:	Applying Stoicism in the Classroom for Complex Needs
57	Chapter 12:	The Stoic influenced lives of well known people
61	Chapter 13:	Integrating Stoicism, Mindfulness, and Health Practices into Educators' Personal Lives
64	Chapter 14:	The Transformative Power of Stoicism for Students
68	Chapter 15:	Strengthening Teacher-Parent Relationships through Stoicism
72	Chapter 16:	Fostering Staff Relationships through Stoicism

76	Chapter 17:	Adopting a Stoic Mindset in School Districts
80	Conclusion	
82	Supplementary Resources	
83	Stoic quotes by Category	
95	Stoic Quotes by Well Know People	
101	Educational Books which may be used in the Stoic Classroom	
102	Breath and Visualisation Work for Personal Practice and Clasroom Practice	
117	Works Cited	

Introduction:

As educators, we face numerous challenges in our profession, from managing classrooms to guiding students through academic and personal growth. Drawing inspiration from the timeless wisdom of Stoic philosophers such as Marcus Aurelius, Seneca, and Epictetus, this book will offer authentic insights and practical teachings to begin your career as an educator, or to simply reinvent yourself as educators. Through a collection of well chosen Stoic quotes and lived experience. I will discuss and explore how the ancient principles of Stoicism can rejuvenate, heal and restore any educator's inner teaching fire. This work will both educate and inspire a new generation and an older ones' concept of resilience, wisdom, and compassion in the next generation coming into our classroom.

In University educators are given the metaphorical golden tickets of what it meant to educate. Many of us were naive about what it actually meant to be an educator. However the average University education often does not fully prepare the newly trained teacher for the sharp realities challenges facing the modern educator. Newly trained Teachers are leaving the profession earlier than ever before. Most don't make it past the five year mark, and the reasons behind this are disturbing and alarming. In 2022 the New

York times was quoted as saying: " In a 2022 survey conducted by the National Education Association, 55 percent of educators said that they were thinking about leaving the profession, many of them citing pandemic-related difficulties and burnout. Teachers must not only face long hours in a stressful environment, but also the rise of political debates around Covid policies and curriculums." (Sejla, 2022)

Large never ending workloads coupled with extra responsibilities, demands for running extracurricular activities along with daily lesson planning, and marking are only some of the demands the new teacher faces . Older teachers similarly face: chronic health issues, depression, workplace toxicity, burnout and sadly due to budget cuts and complex classrooms often have long lost the passion and gumption they once had in the earlier days of their career. Amidst all this strife.. Is there really anything that can be done?

Yes there is..and the ancient stoics had answers! Even, amidst chaos and complex classrooms there are still reasons to be optimistic. There are still joyous moments in everyday teaching and the rewards of witnessing students' growth, we also encounter a myriad of challenges that test our resolve and resilience. Although the journey of an average educator in North America is fraught with obstacles and uncertainties the wisdom of Stoic philosophy offers a guiding light, illuminating the path toward inner peace and professional fulfillment.

Stoicism, with its emphasis on virtue, equanimity, and self-mastery, provides invaluable insights into the challenges we face as educators and offers practical strategies for overcoming them. By integrating Stoic principles into ones teaching practices, coupled with mindfulness and lifestyle improvement; one can cultivate a sense of inner peace and purpose, empowering ourselves and our students to still thrive and shine amid adversity. Through reflection, dialogue, and action, we can embark on a transformative journey of personal and professional development, guided by the timeless wisdom of the Stoic masters!

Chapter 1: Addressing the Challenges in North American Education

"If you want to improve, be content to be thought foolish and stupid." —Epictetus

The state of education in the average North American classroom is brimming with challenges that threaten the well-being of students, teachers, and administrators alike. From large class sizes and overburdened educators to unregulated student behavior and under-resourced programs, the educational landscape is in dire need of support and reform. In this chapter, we examine the pressing issues facing North American education and explore how Stoic philosophy can serve as a powerful tool for navigating through these challenges with resilience, wisdom, and compassion.

Large Class Sizes and Overburdened Educators:

One of the most pressing issues in education is the prevalence of large class sizes and overburdened educators with complex classrooms. Teachers are often tasked with managing classrooms of 35 or more students, making it challenging to provide individualized attention and support. As a result, educators may feel overwhelmed and burned out, leading to or decreased job satisfaction and effectiveness in the classroom. Stoic philosophy offers educators strategies for managing stress, cultivating emotional resilience, and finding purpose and fulfillment in their work despite the challenges they face.

Unregulated Student Behavior and Under-Resourced Programs:

Another significant challenge in North American education is the frequency of unregulated student behavior and under-resourced programs. Many schools lack the resources and support systems needed to address the diverse needs of students, leading to disruptions in the classroom and barriers to learning. Educators may feel ill-equipped to handle challenging behaviors and provide the necessary support for students with special needs. Stoic philosophy offers educators strategies for maintaining composure, responding effectively to difficult situations, and advocating for the resources and support systems needed to create a positive and inclusive learning environment for all students.

Schools in Disrepair and Lack of Training for Special Situations:

In addition to large class sizes and unregulated student behavior, many schools in North America face physical and infrastructural challenges, such as schools in disrepair and a lack of training for special situations. Educators may find themselves navigating through unsafe or inadequate learning environments, further exacerbating the challenges they face in the classroom. Stoic philosophy encourages educators to focus on what is within their control, advocating for change and taking proactive steps to address the challenges they face. By cultivating resilience, adaptability, and resourcefulness, educators can navigate through difficult circumstances and create positive change in their schools and communities.

Conclusion:

In conclusion, the challenges facing North American education are significant, but they are not hopeless. By integrating Stoic philosophy into their personal and professional lives, educators can cultivate resilience, wisdom, and compassion in the face of adversity. Stoicism offers educators practical strategies for managing stress, responding effectively to difficult situations, and advocating for positive change in their schools and communities. As educators, it is possible to harness the power of Stoic philosophy to navigate through the rollercoaster of education with grace and purpose, knowing that by doing so, we can create a brighter future for our students and ourselves.

Chapter 2: Drawing Inspiration from Ancient Greek Stoicism

"How long can you afford to put off who you really want to be? Your nobler self cannot wait any longer. Decide to be extraordinary and do what you need to do now."
—Epictetus

In our ancient world history, the ancient Greeks left behind a rich legacy of philosophy and wisdom that continues to resonate with us today. Among their philosophical schools, Stoicism stands out as a beacon of resilience, offering timeless insights into how we can overcome hardship and face adversity with courage and grace. In this chapter, we'll explore how educators can draw inspiration from ancient Greek Stoicism to navigate the challenges of teaching and find strength in the face of adversity.

The Stoic Way of Life:

The ancient Greek Stoics, including luminaries such as: Epictetus, Seneca, and Marcus Aurelius, and Cato the younger ebraced a philosophy focused on living by nature, cultivating inner tranquility, and embracing adversity as an opportunity for growth. Their teachings emphasized the importance of: virtue, resilience, and acceptance in achieving a life of *eudaimonia* a Greek word literally translating to the state or condition of 'good spirit', and which is commonly translated as 'happiness' or 'welfare'.

Epictetus: From Slave to Philosopher:

Epictetus was born into slavery and faced numerous hardships throughout his life. Despite his circumstances, he embraced Stoic philosophy and focused on what he could control – his thoughts and actions. He famously said, "He is a wise man who does not grieve for the things which he has not, but rejoices for those which he has." (*The Encheiridion* no. 129). Epictetus's teachings emphasize the power of perspective and resilience in the face of adversity. Despite being a slave, he achieved inner freedom through Stoic principles, eventually becoming one of the most influential philosophers of his time.

Seneca: Stoic Statesman and Philosopher:

Seneca served as an advisor to Emperor Nero during a tumultuous period in Roman history. Despite being in a position of power, Seneca remained true to the Stoic virtues of integrity and moral courage. When faced with difficult decisions, he prioritized the well-being of the people over personal gain. Seneca's letters, collected in his work "Letters to Lucilius,"(Seneca, and Barke, 1932) offers timeless wisdom on how to live a virtuous life amidst the challenges of the world. One of Seneca's famous quotes is, "Luck is what happens when preparation meets opportunity,"illustrating his belief in the importance of preparation and resilience in achieving success.

Marcus Aurelius: The Philosopher Emperor:

Marcus Aurelius, often referred to as the philosopher-king, faced numerous challenges during his reign as Emperor of Rome. Despite the demands of his position, he remained committed to Stoic principles and wrote extensively on the nature of virtue and resilience in his "Meditations." Marcus Aurelius believed in the power of rationality and self-discipline in overcoming adversity. He famously said in his Meditations, "You have power over your mind - not outside events. Realize this, and you will find strength." (Aurelius, Book IV, passage 3) Marcus Aurelius's life demonstrates the Stoic ideal of living by nature and maintaining inner peace amidst the chaos of the world.

Cato the Younger: Stoic Senator and Freedom Fighter:

Cato the Younger was a faithful defender of the Roman Republic during a time of political corruption and tyranny. Despite facing opposition and persecution, he remained steadfast in his commitment to the Stoic virtues of honesty and integrity. Cato famously opposed Julius Caesar's rise to power and fought for the principles of liberty and justice until his death. His unwavering courage and moral conviction continue to inspire generations of Stoics and freedom fighters alike.

These personal examples from the lives of ancient Stoics demonstrate how they applied Stoic wisdom to overcome adversity, pursue resilience, and lead lives of meaning and purpose. Through their teachings and actions, they continue to inspire us to embrace Stoic principles in our own lives and work towards for virtue and excellence.

Chapter 3: Building Emotional Resilience in the Educator

"The best answer to anger is silence." —Marcus Aurelius

Amid a chaotic classroom environment, a seasoned teacher versed in the practice of Stoicism can still demonstrate Stoic principles by remaining composed and undisturbed in the face of adversity. Rather than reacting impulsively to disruptive behavior or challenges, they practices the Stoic virtue of emotional resilience, responding with patience and understanding. Through a calm demeanor, mindful breathing practice, and knowledge of stoic principals individual teachers can succeed in creating a supportive learning environment where students feel empowered to succeed.

Teaching students to develop emotional intelligence through the lessons of empathy through practicing familiar social skills scenarios, and self-regulation skills, will develop a culture of both respect and cooperation in the classroom.

Modelling to students how to respond to stressful scenarios with grace, patience and understanding instead of stress and panic; will go a long way in creating a safe and supportive environment where students thrive. Through applying stoic principles students will gain first hand experience that it is possible to navigate through life's ups and downs with grace and dignity, no matter what obstacles may arise.

In the spirit of Stoic philosophy, educators can explore various strategies for managing emotions and maintaining composure in the classroom. By modelling emotional intelligence and self-regulation skills, teachers can create a class culture of respect and cooperation, where students feel valued and supported. The following is a list of suggestions that students can engage in during their school day

- **Practice mindfulness and self-awareness**: Encourage teachers to cultivate mindfulness practices such as deep breathing exercises and meditation to enhance self-awareness and emotional regulation.
- **Develop empathy and understanding**: Teaching educators to empathize with their students' perspectives and experiences, fostering a sense of connection and trust within the classroom community. Practice scenarios could be created on cards and acted out and reflected on by teachers with their peers. Similar scenarios can then be taken to the classroom by the teachers who are now empowered through their own professional development work with empathy.
- **Model resilience and adaptability**: Emphasize the importance of resilience and adaptability in the face of challenges. Encourage teachers to embrace setbacks as opportunities for growth and learning, demonstrating perseverance and determination in their own lives.
- **Promote a positive classroom culture**: Create a supportive and inclusive learning environment where students feel valued and respected. Encourage collaboration and

teamwork, celebrating the unique strengths and contributions of each individual.

By embracing the principles of Stoic philosophy and integrating them into their teaching practices, educators can cultivate emotional resilience and create a nurturing learning environment where students feel empowered to succeed. As Marcus Aurelius wisely said "The best answer to anger is silence."(Aurelius and Hays, 2003) This is a universal reminder of the power of calm composure and self-control in the face of adversity.

Chapter 4: What can I do? Focusing on What's Within Your Control

"You have power over your mind – not outside events. Realize this, and you will find strength."
—Marcus Aurelius

Imagine a first year teacher standing at the front of her classroom at the very start of the year, surrounded by a large group of students. Instead of feeling overwhelmed by this experience, this young teacher might draw on her stoic knowledge, and adopt the Serenity Prayer with their class at the onset of the year. In its simplest form, the serenity prayer is:

"May I have the serenity to accept the things I cannot change,
the courage to change the things I can, and the wisdom to know the
difference." (Sandip, 2022)

Here is another version:

"I am responsible for my own peace,
So, I accept my past.

I'll be brave enough to change my current conditions,

Ignore other people's opinions of me,
And only compare myself to who I was yesterday.

I'll make the most of every moment
While being kind and true to myself
And find my happiness." (Sandip, 2022)

Using the prayer in it's non religious form can be used as a supporting principle in one's teaching philosophy by embracing the Stoic ideals of acceptance and empowerment. By focusing on what is within a student's mind under their control, (such as their attitudes, actions, and responses)—a sense of inner strength and resilience is created.

Rather than becoming overwhelmed by external factors or obstacles, the teacher can maintain a sense of agency and optimism, inspiring their students to adopt the same ideals of acceptance and empowerment, recognizing that true strength lies in focusing on what is within one's control in the present moment.

Encouraging students to know the difference between what they can and cannot control, by empowering them to focus their efforts on areas within their influence. Foster a growth mindset and a sense of personal responsibility, teaching students to approach challenges with courage and determination. Additionally educators can discover helpful insights on how to navigate through life's complexities by modelling both resilience and clarity. Central to Stoic philosophy is the notion of *focusing on what is within our control*—a principle that holds particular relevance in the field of education.

Teaching Reflection: Empowering Students

Incorporating Stoic principles into the classroom, educators can empower students to differentiate between what they can and cannot control, fostering a sense of agency and resilience. Through reflective exercises and discussions, teachers can encourage students to:

- **Identify areas of daily life within their control:** Prompt students to reflect on aspects of their lives that they have the power to influence, such as their attitudes, behaviors, and choices.
- **Cultivate a growth mindset:** Teach students to embrace challenges as opportunities for growth and learning, rather than obstacles to be feared or avoided.
- **Foster personal responsibility:** Encourage students to take ownership of their actions and decisions, recognizing that they have the power to shape their destinies.
- **Develop coping strategies:** Provide students with tools and techniques for managing stress and adversity, such as mindfulness practices, goal-setting strategies, and positive self-talk.

By infusing these principles of Stoic philosophy in their students, educators can supply them with the mindset and skills needed to thrive in an ever-changing world. As Marcus Aurelius reminds us in the Meditations, "You have power over your mind – not outside events." (Aurelius, Book IV, passage 3) Through focused attention and intentional action, students can cultivate inner strength and resilience, empowering them to navigate through life's challenges with confidence and grace.

Chapter 5: Being Authentic through Virtue and Integrity

"Waste no more time arguing about what a good man should be. Be one." —Marcus Aurelius

An ideal Stoic trained educator embodies Stoic virtues such as: integrity, honesty, and moral courage in their interactions with students and colleagues. Rather than merely espousing ethical principles, they lead by example, demonstrating integrity and authenticity in her words and actions. Through their unwavering commitment to virtue, they inspire others to strive for excellence and ethical conduct, creating a culture of trust and respect within the school community.

Fostering character development and ethical reasoning in students, emphasizing the importance of integrity and moral courage. Provide opportunities for students to engage in ethical discussions and dilemmas, guiding them toward a deeper understanding of virtue and its practical application in their lives.

In the pursuit of excellence and moral clarity, Stoic philosophy offers invaluable guidance on the importance of embracing virtue and integrity. Educators play a pivotal role in shaping the ethical compasses of our students, guiding them towards lives of purpose and integrity. Inspired by the wisdom of Marcus Aurelius and other Stoic thinkers, educators can explore the significance of leading by example and fostering a culture of virtue within the school community.

Imagine a school where integrity and honesty are not merely discussed, but actually lived out each day by its faculty and staff. At the heart of this vision stands an ideal education. A Stoic school should implement virtues such as: integrity, honesty, and moral courage. Rather than simply lecturing students on the importance of ethical conduct, all educators should lead by using personal examples, that demonstrate a commitment to these wise principles through authenticity in all aspects of one's life.

Whether faced with difficult decisions or ethical dilemmas, lead stoic teachers should model to colleagues and students doing what is right. Through these positive actions, others follow suit, fostering a culture of trust and respect within the school community.

Reading lists and curriculum should be developed with resources and authors who embody this philosophy. See the end of this book for a list of books and sources used in this book you can use directly in the classroom with individual lessons.

Fostering Virtue in Students

Through our role as educators, we have the power to shape the moral character and ethical reasoning of our students. By incorporating Stoic principles of virtue and integrity into our teaching practices, we can empower students to become ethical leaders and responsible citizens. Here are some strategies for fostering virtue in students:

- Emphasize the importance of integrity: Teach students the value of honesty, authenticity, and moral courage in all aspects of their lives.
- Provide opportunities for ethical discussions: Engage students in thought-provoking conversations about moral dilemmas and ethical decision-making, encouraging them to reflect on their values and principles.
- Lead by example: Demonstrate integrity and ethical conduct in your interactions with students and colleagues, serving as a positive role model for ethical behavior.
- Encourage self-reflection: Prompt students to examine their own actions and motivations, fostering self-awareness and moral discernment.

Through these Stoic teaching based teaching methodolohies and the support of schools, educators can instill in students a deep appreciation for virtue and integrity, equipping them with the moral compass they need to navigate life's complexities with wisdom and grace. By embodying Stoic virtues in our own lives and inspiring others to do the same, we can create a world where integrity and ethical conduct are cherished above all else.

Chapter 6: Stoic Principles for Teachers

"Never let the future disturb you. You will meet it, if you have to, with the same weapons of reason which today arm you against the present." —Marcus Aurelius

Stoic principles can serve as invaluable tools for teachers, helping them navigate the complexities of their career with grace, resilience, and wisdom. The following is a list of stoic principles that individual teachers can implement into their own own lives; to not only make them better teachers, but also better humans.

1. Focus on What You Can Control:

Stoicism teaches us to focus our energy on the things within our control and accept those that are not. As a teacher, it's easy to become overwhelmed by external factors such as administrative policies, student behaviors, or societal pressures. However, dwelling on these things only leads to frustration and burnout.

Instead, focus on aspects of your teaching that you can control, such as your preparation, lesson delivery, and classroom environment. By directing your efforts towards these areas, you'll feel more empowered and effective in your role as an educator.

2. Embrace Challenges as Opportunities for Growth:

Stoicism encourages us to view challenges as opportunities for growth rather than obstacles to success. As a teacher, you will inevitably encounter difficulties - whether it's a disruptive student, a difficult parent, or a curriculum change.

Instead of becoming disheartened, approach these challenges with a stoic mindset. Ask yourself what you can learn from the experience and how you can use it to become a better teacher. By reframing setbacks as opportunities for personal and professional development, you'll cultivate resilience and adaptability in your teaching practice.

3. Practice Virtue in Your Interactions:

Stoicism emphasizes the importance of virtue - qualities such as wisdom, courage, justice, and temperance. As a teacher, embodying these virtues in your interactions with students, colleagues, and parents can profoundly impact your effectiveness and influence.

Practice wisdom by continually seeking to improve your teaching methods and pedagogical knowledge. Demonstrate courage by advocating for your students' needs and standing up for what you believe is right. Uphold justice by treating all students fairly and equitably, regardless of their background or abilities. Finally, exercise temperance by maintaining composure and patience, even in challenging situations.

4. Cultivate Inner Tranquility:

Stoicism teaches us to cultivate inner tranquility amidst the chaos of life. As a teacher, maintaining a sense of calm and equanimity is essential for fostering a positive learning environment and effectively managing classroom dynamics.

Practice mindfulness and self-reflection to become more aware of your thoughts and emotions. When faced with stress or frustration, take a moment to pause, breathe, and regain perspective. Remember that you have the power to choose how you respond to situations, and cultivating inner peace will enable you to respond with clarity and compassion.

5. Focus on the Greater Good:

Just like the sacred, wisdom teachings of our Indigenous elders, Stoicism also reminds us of our connection to all of humanity and the importance of doing the right thing. When you choose a career in teaching, you have the privilege and responsibility to shape the minds and hearts of future generations.

Focus on the impact you can have on your students' lives, both academically and personally. Strive to instill in them a love of learning, critical thinking skills, and a sense of empathy and compassion for others. By dedicating yourself to the noble pursuit of education, you contribute to the betterment of society as a whole.

Incorporating Stoic principles into your teaching practice can lead to greater resilience, effectiveness, and fulfillment in your career as an educator. By focusing on what you can control, embracing challenges as opportunities for growth, practicing virtue in your interactions, cultivating inner tranquility, and focusing on the greater good, you can navigate the complexities of teaching with wisdom, grace, and purpose.

Chapter 7: Cultivating Stoic-Based Meditations for Daily Practice

"Very little is needed to make a happy life; it is all within yourself, in your way of thinking." —Marcus Aurelius

In the fast-paced world of education, cultivating a sense of inner calm and resilience is essential for navigating the challenges of the profession. Stoic-based meditations offer powerful techniques for educators to cultivate mindfulness, emotional resilience, and wisdom in their daily lives. In this chapter, we will explore how educators can integrate Stoic-based meditations into their personal practice, providing specific suggestions and techniques for incorporating Stoic principles into daily life.

1. Morning Reflections:

Practice Suggestions:

- Begin each morning with a Stoic reflection on the day ahead. Reflect on Stoic principles such as: acceptance, virtue, and resilience, setting intentions to embody these qualities throughout the day.
- Journal about your goals and priorities for the day, focusing on what is within your control and letting go of concerns about external events.
- Practice gratitude by reflecting on the things you are thankful for in your own life, cultivating a sense of appreciation and contentment.

2. Mindful Breathing Exercises:

Practice Suggestions:

- Take a few minutes throughout the day to engage in mindful breathing exercises. Focus on your breath as it enters and leaves your body, bringing your attention back to the present moment whenever your mind wanders.
- As you inhale, silently repeat a Stoic mantra such as "I can accept what is" or "I am a virtuous person." As you exhale, release any tension or stress you may be holding onto, cultivating a sense of calm and easing tension.

3. Evening Reflections:

Practice Suggestions:

- Before bed, engage in an evening reflection practice inspired by Stoic philosophy. Review the events of the day with a spirit of curiosity and self-awareness, acknowledging both your successes and areas for growth.
- Practice the Stoic exercise of **"premeditatio malorum"** (*premeditation of evils*) by envisioning potential challenges or setbacks you may encounter in the future. Reflect on how you can respond to these challenges with wisdom and resilience, preparing yourself mentally and emotionally for whatever may come.

4. Stoic Reading and Contemplation:

Practice Suggestions:

- Set aside time each day to read and reflect on Stoic texts, such as the works of Marcus Aurelius, Seneca, and Epictetus. Choose passages that resonate with you and contemplate their meaning in relation to your own life and experiences.
- Keep a *Stoic journal* where you can record your reflections on Stoic principles and how you are applying them in your daily life. Write down insights, challenges, and moments of growth, cultivating a deeper understanding of Stoic philosophy and its practical applications.

Integrating Stoic-based mindfulness practice into a daily personal practice offers educators powerful tools for cultivating mindfulness, emotional resilience, and wisdom in their lives. By incorporating Stoic principles into morning reflections, mindful breathing exercises, evening reflections, and contemplative reading practices, educators can nurture a sense of inner calm and strength that empowers them to navigate the challenges of the profession with grace and integrity. Through consistent practice and self-reflection, educators can cultivate a deeper connection to Stoic philosophy and its transformative potential in their lives.

Chapter 8: Practical Applications of Stoicism in the Classroom

"The whole future lies in uncertainty: live immediately."
—Seneca

Stoic philosophy is not merely a set of abstract principles—it is a practical guide for living a life of virtue and wisdom. In this chapter, we will explore how educators can apply Stoic teachings in the classroom to foster resilience, cultivate critical thinking skills, and nurture a positive learning environment. Through a series of practical strategies and exercises, we empower educators to integrate Stoicism into their teaching practices and inspire students to lead lives of purpose and fulfillment.

Embracing Stoic Mindfulness:

One of the core tenets of Stoicism is the practice of mindfulness—the ability to remain present and aware of our thoughts, emotions, and actions. Educators can incorporate Stoic mindfulness techniques into the classroom to help students develop self-awareness and emotional regulation. Simple practices such as mindful breathing exercises, gratitude journaling, and reflection can empower students to navigate through challenges with clarity and composure.

Teaching Resilience through Stoic Virtues:

Stoic virtues such as courage, temperance, and wisdom serve as pillars of strength in the face of adversity. By teaching students about these virtues and encouraging them to embody them in their daily lives, educators can instill a sense of resilience and determination. Role-playing exercises, group discussions, and real-life examples can help students understand the practical applications of Stoic virtues and empower them to overcome obstacles with grace and fortitude.

Fostering Stoic Ethics and Moral Reasoning:

Stoic philosophy emphasizes the importance of ethical conduct and moral reasoning. Educators can engage students in ethical discussions and dilemmas, challenging them to apply Stoic principles to real-world scenarios. By encouraging critical thinking and ethical reflection, educators empower students to make informed and virtuous decisions in their personal and academic lives.

Creating a Stoic Classroom Culture:

Lastly, educators can cultivate a Stoic-inspired classroom culture characterized by resilience, empathy, and collaboration. By modeling Stoic virtues and principles in their interactions with students and colleagues, educators set a positive example for their students to follow. Through consistent reinforcement and encouragement, educators can create an environment where students feel supported, empowered, and inspired to live a life of purpose and integrity.

Chapter 9: Winning Over Parents and Students

"Don't explain your philosophy. Embody it." —Epictetus

Stoicism isn't just for the classroom—it's a philosophy that can profoundly impact every aspect of our lives. In this chapter, we explore how educators can effectively communicate the principles of Stoicism to parents and students, empowering them to embrace Stoic virtues both inside and outside the classroom. By highlighting the practical benefits of Stoicism and providing actionable strategies for implementation, educators can inspire parents and students to adopt Stoic principles in their daily lives and reap the rewards of resilience, wisdom, and inner peace.

Benefits of Stoicism for Parents:

Parents face a complex network of challenges as they navigate the complexities of raising children and managing family life. By introducing parents to the principles of Stoicism, educators can provide them with valuable tools for navigating through the ups and downs of parenthood with grace and resilience. From managing stress and cultivating patience to fostering emotional intelligence in their children, Stoicism offers practical strategies for parents to enhance their parenting skills and create a harmonious family environment.

Empowering Students with Stoic Principles:

For students, the pressures of academic performance, social dynamics, and personal growth can be overwhelming. By introducing Stoic philosophy into the curriculum, educators can empower students with the mindset and tools they need to navigate through life's challenges with confidence and resilience. Through discussions, activities, and real-life examples, students can learn to cultivate emotional intelligence, develop critical thinking skills, and build a strong sense of self-efficacy—all essential components of a well-rounded education.

Creating a Stoic Community:

By fostering a sense of community and collaboration among parents, students, and educators, schools can create an environment where Stoic principles are valued and embraced by all members of the community. Through workshops, seminars, and parent-teacher meetings, educators can provide parents and students with opportunities to learn about Stoicism and explore its practical applications in their lives. By working together, parents, students, and educators can create a supportive and nurturing environment where Stoic virtues such as resilience, wisdom, and compassion flourish.

Stoicism offers invaluable insights and practical strategies for parents and students alike to navigate through life's challenges with resilience, wisdom, and inner peace. By effectively communicating the principles of Stoicism to parents and students, educators can empower them to embrace Stoic virtues both inside and outside the classroom, creating a ripple effect of positive change in their lives and in the world around them. As educators, let us continue to inspire and empower parents and students with the transformative power of Stoicism, knowing that by doing so, we can make a profound difference in the lives of those we touch.

Chapter 10: Practical Integration of Stoicism into Classroom Activities

"If a man knows not to which port he sails, no wind is favorable."

—Seneca

Incorporating Stoic principles into classroom activities not only enhances academic learning but also cultivates important life skills such as resilience, emotional intelligence, and critical thinking. In this chapter, we'll explore effective activities and lesson plans that seamlessly integrate Stoicism into the classroom, providing students with practical tools for personal growth and development.

Activity 1: Stoic Journaling

Objective: Encourage students to reflect on Stoic principles and apply them to their daily lives through journaling.

Instructions:

- Provide students with prompts based on Stoic quotes or principles (e.g., "What is within your control today?" or "How can you practice acceptance in challenging situations?")
- Ask students to write daily journal entries reflecting on their thoughts, emotions, and actions in light of Stoic teachings.
- Encourage students to share insights and experiences with their peers, fostering a sense of community and support.

Example Stoic Quote: "Happiness and freedom begin with a clear understanding of one principle: Some things are within our control, and some things are not." - Epictetus

Activity 2: Stoic Reflections on Literature

Objective: Analyze literary texts through a Stoic lens to deepen understanding and foster critical thinking.

Instructions:

- Select a passage from a literary work that resonates with Stoic themes (e.g., resilience, acceptance, virtue). See the list of resources at the end of this book.
- Guide students in analyzing the passage and identifying Stoic principles embedded within the text.
- Facilitate a discussion on how characters demonstrate Stoic virtues and how their actions align with Stoic philosophy.
- Encourage students to apply Stoic insights to their own lives and experiences, drawing parallels between the text and their personal journey.

Example Stoic Quote: "The happiness of your life depends upon the quality of your thoughts." - Marcus Aurelius

2. Separate Lessons and Activities on Stoicism:

Activity 3: Stoic Role Models

Objective: Introduce students to historical and contemporary figures who exemplify Stoic virtues and inspire personal growth.

Instructions:

- Provide students with biographical information about Stoic role models such as Marcus Aurelius, Epictetus, or Seneca.
- Facilitate a discussion on the key principles and teachings of Stoicism embodied by these individuals.
- Encourage students to reflect on how they can emulate Stoic role models in their own lives and aspire to cultivate similar virtues.
- Invite students to research and present on other figures who embody Stoic principles, fostering a deeper understanding and appreciation of Stoicism.

Example Stoic Quote: "Waste no more time arguing about what a good man should be. Be one." - Marcus Aurelius

Activity 4: Stoic Mindfulness Meditation

Objective: Introduce students to Stoic mindfulness practices to cultivate inner tranquility and emotional resilience.

Instructions:

- Guide students through a mindfulness meditation focused on Stoic themes such as acceptance, impermanence, and gratitude.
- Encourage students to observe their thoughts and emotions with non-judgmental awareness, acknowledging them without attachment or aversion.
- Facilitate a discussion on the experience of mindfulness meditation and its relevance to Stoic philosophy.
- Provide resources for students to continue practicing Stoic mindfulness meditation independently, empowering them to integrate these practices into their daily lives.

Example Stoic Quote: "You have power over your mind - not outside events. Realize this, and you will find strength." - Marcus Aurelius

Integrating Stoicism into classroom activities offers students valuable opportunities to engage with timeless wisdom and develop essential life skills. Whether through everyday integration in lessons or separate lessons and activities focused specifically on Stoicism, students can gain insights and tools for personal growth, resilience, and well-being. By incorporating Stoic principles into their educational journey, students not only enhance their academic learning, but also lays a foundation for a fulfilling and meaningful life.

Chapter 11: Applying Stoicism in the Classroom for Complex Needs

"It's not what happens to you, but how you react that matters."
—Epictetus

In the diverse landscape of education, teachers often encounter students with varying needs and backgrounds, including those with trauma, English as a second language (EASL), and students with disabiliites. Stoic philosophy offers valuable insights and practical strategies for supporting these students in their academic and personal growth. In this chapter, we'll explore how Stoicism can be applied in the classroom to meet the needs of diverse learners, with specific examples tailored to students with complex trauma, English as a second language, and disabilities.

1. Supporting Students with Complex Trauma:

Students who have experienced complex trauma may struggle with emotional regulation, trust issues, and difficulty forming relationships. Stoic principles can provide a framework for building resilience and coping with adversity.

Example: Stoic Mindfulness Exercises

- Teach students mindfulness techniques inspired by Stoic philosophy, such as focusing on the present moment and accepting thoughts and emotions without judgment.
- Guide students in journaling about their thoughts and feelings, encouraging them to reflect on Stoic concepts like acceptance and impermanence.
- Provide opportunities for group discussions where students can share their experiences and insights, fostering a sense of community and support.

2. Empowering EASL Students:

English as a second language students may face challenges in language acquisition and cultural adjustment. Stoic philosophy offers strategies for building confidence, overcoming obstacles, and embracing the learning process.

Example: Stoic Language Learning Strategies

- Encourage EASL students to adopt a growth mindset, emphasizing the importance of effort and perseverance in language acquisition.
- Teach students Stoic techniques for managing frustration and maintaining motivation, such as breaking tasks into manageable steps and celebrating small victories.
- Incorporate Stoic themes and stories into everyday language lessons, providing their cultural context and inspiring students to connect with ancient wisdom while learning English.

3. Supporting Students with Disabilities:

Students with disabilities may encounter barriers to learning and participation in the classroom. Stoic principles can empower these students to cultivate resilience, adaptability, and self-advocacy.

Example: Stoic Problem-Solving Strategies

- Teach students problem-solving techniques inspired by Stoic philosophy, such as reframing challenges as opportunities for growth and focusing on solutions rather than obstacles.
- Provide students with tools and resources for self-advocacy, such as communication strategies and assistive technologies, empowering them to express their needs and navigate academic and social environments effectively.
- Foster a supportive and inclusive classroom culture where students with disabilities feel valued and respected, emphasizing the importance of empathy, compassion, and cooperation among classmates.

Stoicism offers valuable insights and practical strategies for supporting diverse learners in the classroom, including those living with complex trauma, EASL, and disabilities. By incorporating Stoic principles into teaching practices and providing students with opportunities to apply these concepts in their academic and personal lives, educators can empower all students to thrive and succeed, regardless of their background or circumstances. Through the cultivation of resilience, adaptability, and self-awareness, students can develop the skills and mindset needed to overcome challenges, embrace opportunities, and live a life of meaning and fulfillment.

Chapter 12: The Stoic influenced lives of well known people

"Once you make a decision, the universe conspires to make it happen." —Ralph Waldo Emerson

While Stoicism may seem like an ancient philosophy, its principles remain relevant and applicable in the modern world. In this chapter, we explore how some of today's most prominent celebrities have embraced Stoicism to navigate through life's challenges and cultivate resilience, wisdom, and inner peace. Through their stories, we gain insight into how Stoic philosophy can inspire and empower individuals from all walks of life, including those in the public eye

Dwayne "The Rock" Johnson:

One of the most recognizable figures in Hollywood, Dwayne "The Rock" Johnson has openly discussed his understanding of Stoic principles in his personal and professional life. Known for his relentless work ethic and unwavering positive attitude, Johnson credits Stoicism with helping him overcome setbacks and maintain a sense of perspective even dealing with the pressures of fame. By focusing on what is within his control and embracing challenges as opportunities for growth, Johnson exemplifies the Stoic ideal of resilience in the face of adversity.

Kristen Bell:

Actress Kristen Bell has spoken candidly about her struggles with anxiety and the role that Stoicism has played in helping her manage her mental health. By practicing mindfulness and acceptance, Bell has learned to cultivate a sense of inner peace and resilience, even in the midst of life's uncertainties. Through her advocacy for mental health awareness and her embrace of Stoic philosophy, Bell serves as an inspiring example of courage and vulnerability in the public eye.

Arnold Schwarzenegger:

Former bodybuilder, actor, and politician Arnold Schwarzenegger is another prominent advocate for Stoic philosophy. Throughout his career, Schwarzenegger has faced numerous challenges and setbacks, from career transitions to personal struggles. By adopting Stoic principles such as discipline, perseverance, and self-mastery, Schwarzenegger has overcome adversity and achieved success in multiple arenas. His commitment to Stoicism serves as a reminder that resilience and determination are key ingredients for achieving one's goals, no matter the obstacles.

The stories of Dwayne "The Rock" Johnson, Kristen Bell, Arnold Schwarzenegger, and other celebrities demonstrate the enduring relevance and practicality of Stoic philosophy in the modern world. Through their examples, we see how Stoicism can empower individuals to navigate through life's challenges with resilience, wisdom, and grace. As educators, we can draw inspiration from these stories and incorporate Stoic principles into our teaching practices, fostering a culture of strength, resilience, and compassion in ourselves and our students. Just as these celebrities have found solace and guidance in Stoicism, so too can we discover its transformative power in our own lives.

Chapter 13: Integrating Stoicism, Mindfulness, and Health Practices into Educators' Personal Lives

"The greatest weapon against stress is out ability to choose one thought over another." —William James

As educators, we dedicate our lives to the noble pursuit of enriching the minds and hearts of our students. Yet, amidst the demands of the profession, it's essential not to overlook our own well-being and personal growth. In this chapter, we explore how educators can integrate Stoic philosophy, mindfulness, and health practices into their personal lives to cultivate resilience, balance, and fulfillment. By prioritizing self-care and adopting holistic approaches to well-being, educators can enhance their effectiveness in the classroom and lead more fulfilling lives.

Stoicism for Educators:

Stoic philosophy offers invaluable insights into how educators can navigate through the challenges and uncertainties of their profession with grace and resilience. By embracing Stoic principles such as focusing on what is within our control, cultivating emotional resilience, and practicing gratitude, educators can cultivate a sense of inner peace and purpose amidst the demands of their work. Through reflection, journaling, and contemplation, educators can integrate Stoicism into their daily lives and lead with clarity and integrity.

Personal Mindfulness Practices for Educators:

Mindfulness practices such as meditation, deep breathing exercises, and mindful movement offer educators powerful tools for managing stress, enhancing focus, and promoting emotional well-being. By incorporating mindfulness into their daily routines, educators can cultivate present-moment awareness and develop greater resilience in the face of adversity. Through mindfulness practices, educators can enhance their ability to connect with themselves and their students on a deeper level, fostering empathy, compassion, and authenticity in their interactions.

Prioritizing Personal Health and Well-being:

In the fast-paced world of education, it's essential for educators to prioritize their physical health and well-being. Regular exercise, nutritious eating habits, and adequate sleep are essential components of a healthy lifestyle that can help educators manage stress, boost energy levels, and enhance overall well-being. By making self-care a priority and incorporating health-promoting practices into their daily lives, educators can sustain their passion for teaching and lead more balanced and fulfilling lives.

In conclusion, integrating Stoicism, mindfulness, and health practices into their personal lives can empower educators to thrive both personally and professionally. By cultivating resilience, mindfulness, and well-being, educators can enhance their effectiveness in the classroom, foster stronger connections with their students, and lead more fulfilling lives. As educators, let us prioritize self-care and personal growth, knowing that by investing in ourselves, we can better serve our students and create a positive impact in the world around us.

Chapter 14: The Transformative Power of Stoicism for Students

"You have a mind-Yes. Well, why not use it? Isn't that all you want-for it to do its job?—Marcus Aurelius

Education is not merely about feeding students knowledge; it's about shaping the character and perspective of individuals. In the realm of personal development, Stoicism offers profound insights and practical wisdom that can deeply impact students' lives. In this chapter, we'll explore how an understanding of Stoicism can transform the lives of students, guiding them towards resilience, wisdom, and inner peace.

1. Building Resilience in the Face of Adversity:

Stoicism teaches us to accept the inevitability of adversity and to develop resilience in its face. For students, this means learning to navigate the challenges of academic life and personal growth with courage and fortitude. As Marcus Aurelius wrote, "The impediment to action advances action. What stands in the way becomes the way."

By embracing obstacles as opportunities for growth rather than as insurmountable barriers, students can cultivate a mindset of resilience that empowers them to overcome setbacks and thrive in the face of adversity.

2. Cultivating Emotional Intelligence and Self-Mastery:

Stoicism emphasizes the importance of mastering one's emotions and cultivating inner tranquility. In a world filled with distractions and uncertainties, this skill is invaluable for students navigating the complexities of adolescence and young adulthood.

As Epictetus famously said, "We cannot choose our external circumstances, but we can always choose how we respond to them."(Epictetus, Manual For Living 17) By teaching students to observe and question their own repetitive thoughts and emotions with mindfulness and self-awareness, Stoicism equips them with the tools to respond to life's challenges with equanimity and grace.

3. Fostering a Sense of Purpose and Meaning:

Stoicism invites students to contemplate the deeper questions of existence and to cultivate a sense of purpose and meaning in their lives. As Seneca wrote, "If a man knows not to which port he sails, no wind is favorable." (Seneca, Letters from a Stoic, 92) By encouraging students to reflect on their values, goals, and aspirations, Stoicism helps them chart a course towards a life of meaning and fulfillment.

Whether it's through the pursuit of academic excellence, the cultivation of meaningful relationships, or the service to others, Stoicism inspires students to live with intention and purpose, guiding them towards a life of significance and fulfillment.

4. Fostering Empathy and Compassion:

Stoicism emphasizes the interconnectedness of humanity and the importance of compassion and empathy towards others. As Marcus Aurelius wrote in his Meditations, "What is not good for the beehive, cannot be good for the bees." (Aurelius, Meditations Book 9, Section 2) We see that by cultivating a sense of empathy and compassion, students learn to recognize the inherent dignity and worth of every individual, fostering a more inclusive and compassionate society.

Through acts of kindness, generosity, and service to others, students embody the principles of Stoicism in action, creating ripple effects of positive change that extend far beyond themselves.

An understanding of Stoicism has the power to profoundly transform the lives of students, guiding them towards resilience, wisdom, and inner peace. By building resilience in the face of adversity, cultivating emotional intelligence and self-mastery, fostering a sense of purpose and meaning, and fostering empathy and compassion, Stoicism equips students with the tools they need to navigate the complexities of life with courage, grace, and integrity.

Chapter 15: Strengthening Teacher-Parent Relationships through Stoicism

"Of all natures's gifts to the human race, what is sweeter to a man than his children?" —Marcus Tullius Cicero

Effective communication between teachers and parents is essential for student success. However, maintaining positive relationships with parents can be challenging, especially when faced with differing expectations or communication barriers. In this chapter, we'll explore how an understanding of Stoicism can also transform and enhance the relationships between teachers and parents, fostering mutual respect, understanding, and cooperation.

1. Practicing Empathy and Understanding:

Stoicism teaches us to empathize with others and seek to understand their perspectives. For teachers, this means recognizing that parents come from diverse backgrounds and may have their own unique concerns and priorities regarding their child's education. As Marcus Aurelius wrote is his meditations, By approaching interactions with parents with an open heart and mind, teachers can cultivate empathy and understanding, laying the foundation for positive and productive relationships.

2. Focusing on Effective Communication:

Stoicism emphasizes the importance of clear and effective communication in fostering harmonious relationships. For teachers and parents, this means communicating openly and honestly, expressing concerns or feedback respectfully, and actively listening to one another's perspectives. As Epictetus wrote, "We have two ears and one mouth so that we can listen twice as much as we speak." (Crossley and Epictetus, 1909)

By prioritizing active listening and empathetic communication, teachers and parents can bridge gaps in understanding and work together towards shared goals for the benefit of the student.

3. Cultivating Patience and Resilience:

Stoicism teaches us to remain calm and composed in the face of challenges and setbacks. For teachers, this means cultivating patience and resilience when dealing with difficult or confrontational parents. As Seneca wrote, "We suffer more often in imagination than in reality."

By reframing challenging situations as opportunities for growth and learning, teachers can maintain a sense of equanimity and respond to parent concerns with grace and professionalism.

4. Fostering Collaboration and Partnership:

Stoicism emphasizes the importance of working together towards common goals and objectives. For teachers and parents, this means viewing each other as partners in the educational journey of the child. As Marcus Aurelius wrote in the Meditations: "The best revenge is to be unlike him who performed the injury."(Aurelius, Book 9, section 14)

By fostering a spirit of collaboration and partnership, teachers and parents can leverage their respective strengths and expertise to support the holistic development of the student, creating a cohesive and supportive educational environment.

An understanding of Stoicism can transform and enhance the relationships between teachers and parents, fostering mutual respect, understanding, and cooperation. By practicing empathy and understanding, focusing on effective communication, cultivating patience and resilience, and fostering collaboration and partnership, teachers and parents can work together towards shared goals for the benefit of the student.

Chapter 16: Fostering Staff Relationships through Stoicism

"In prosperity it is very easy to find a friend; but in adversity it is the most difficult of all things." —Epictetus

A strong and supportive staff is the backbone of a successful school community. However, building and maintaining positive relationships among colleagues can be challenging, especially in the fast-paced and demanding environment of education. In this chapter, we'll explore how an understanding of Stoicism can assist with staff relationships within a school, promoting collaboration, mutual respect, and a shared sense of purpose.

1. Embracing Virtue and Integrity:

Stoicism emphasizes the importance of virtue and integrity in all aspects of life, including professional relationships. For staff members, this means embodying qualities such as honesty, fairness, and respect in their interactions with colleagues. As Seneca wrote, "Virtue is nothing else than right reason."

By prioritizing virtue and integrity, staff members can cultivate a culture of trust and mutual respect within the school community, laying the foundation for strong and harmonious relationships.

2. Practicing Empathy and Understanding:

Stoicism encourages us to empathize with others and seek to understand their perspectives. For staff members, this means recognizing the unique challenges and experiences of their colleagues and offering support and encouragement when needed. As Marcus Aurelius wrote, "Everything we hear is an opinion, not a fact. Everything we see is a perspective, not the truth."

By practicing empathy and understanding, staff members can foster a sense of camaraderie and solidarity, strengthening their bonds as colleagues and friends.

3. Cultivating Resilience and Adaptability:

Stoicism teaches us to remain resilient and adaptable in the face of adversity and change. For staff members, this means embracing challenges as opportunities for growth and learning, rather than as obstacles to success. As Epictetus wrote, "It's not what happens to you, but how you react to it that matters."

By cultivating resilience and adaptability, staff members can navigate the complexities of the school environment with grace and composure, inspiring confidence and trust among their colleagues.

4. Suggesting Team Building Exercises Inspired by Stoicism:

a. **The Stoic Circle of Control:** Divide staff members into small groups and ask them to identify aspects of their work that are within their control (e.g., attitude, effort, communication) and those that are not (e.g., external policies, decisions made by higher authorities). Encourage them to brainstorm strategies for focusing their energy on what they can control and letting go of what they cannot.

b. **The Stoic Gratitude Journal**: Invite staff members to keep a gratitude journal where they write down three things they're grateful for each day. Encourage them to reflect on how practicing gratitude can help cultivate resilience and a positive outlook, even in challenging times.

c. **The Stoic Role Model Reflection**: Ask staff members to identify a historical or contemporary figure who embodies Stoic principles (e.g., Marcus Aurelius, Epictetus, Nelson Mandela) and share how their example inspires them in their own professional lives. Encourage them to discuss how they can apply the lessons learned from their chosen role model to improve their relationships with colleagues and enhance their effectiveness as educators.

An understanding of Stoicism can assist with staff relationships within a school, promoting collaboration, mutual respect, and a shared sense of purpose. By embracing virtue and integrity, practicing empathy and understanding, cultivating resilience and adaptability, and engaging in team-building exercises inspired by Stoic principles, staff members can foster a supportive and informed school community where everyone is not just surviving, but thriving!

Chapter 17: Adopting a Stoic Mindset in School Districts

"Seek not the good in external things; seek it in yourselves." —Epictetus

In the pursuit of holistic education, school districts play a pivotal role in shaping the academic, social, and emotional development of students. By adopting a Stoic mindset at the district level, educators can create a culture that promotes emotional resilience, fosters virtue and character, and encourages a growth mindset among students and staff alike. In this chapter, we'll explore how school districts can integrate Stoic principles into their educational systems, empowering students to navigate life's challenges with courage, wisdom, and resilience.

Integrating Stoic Principles in Educational Systems:

Promoting Emotional Resilience:
- Teach students to recognize and manage their emotions effectively, drawing on Stoic practices such as mindfulness meditation and journaling to cultivate inner tranquility and resilience.
- Introduce mindfulness programs and activities into the curriculum, providing students with practical tools for managing stress and enhancing emotional well-being.
- Offer professional development opportunities for educators to learn about Stoic principles and incorporate them into their teaching practices, creating a supportive environment where students feel empowered to express themselves and seek support when needed.

Fostering Virtue and Character:
- Instill in students the importance of virtue and integrity, drawing inspiration from Stoic role models such as Socrates, who exemplified moral courage and ethical conduct.
- Incorporate character education programs and initiatives that emphasize Stoic virtues such as wisdom, courage, temperance, and justice.
- Celebrate acts of kindness, compassion, and empathy within the school community, reinforcing the value of virtuous behavior and its positive impact on individuals and society as a whole.

Encouraging Growth Mindset:

- Emphasize the power of a growth mindset in fostering academic success and personal development, echoing the Stoic belief in the potential for continuous improvement and self-mastery.
- Provide students with opportunities to set goals, embrace challenges, and learn from setbacks, fostering a sense of resilience and self-efficacy.
- Create a culture of feedback and reflection, where students are encouraged to seek constructive criticism and view failures as opportunities for growth and learning.

The ancient Greek Stoics offer an ageless blueprint for navigating life's challenges with courage, wisdom, and resilience. By adopting a Stoic mindset in school districts, educators can empower themselves and their students to overcome adversity and cultivate a life of meaning and fulfillment. By including Stoic principles in education, school districts can promote a community of learners who not only embrace challenges as opportunities for growth but also can actively demonstrate the virtues of wisdom, courage, and compassion. Through intentional efforts to promote emotional resilience, foster virtue and character, and encourage a growth mindset, school districts can create a nurturing and supportive environment where all students can thrive academically, socially, and emotionally.

Conclusion:

As educators, we hold a great responsibility to not only provide knowledge but also to nurture the character and well-being of our students. Through the exploration of Stoic philosophy in this book, we have uncovered a wealth of enduring wisdom and hands-on insights that can greatly impact our teaching practices and the lives of our students. From cultivating emotional resilience to fostering virtue and integrity, the principles of Stoicism offer vital guidance for navigating the complexities of the classroom with grace and purpose.

In the preceding chapters, we delved into the core principles of Stoicism and explored their practical applications in the educational setting. We learned how to cultivate emotional resilience through mindfulness practices, empower students to embody Stoic virtues, and foster ethical reasoning and moral courage. By integrating these teachings into our teaching practices, we have the power to create a transformative learning environment where students feel supported, inspired, and empowered to reach their full potential.

Stoic philosophy reminds us that we have the power to shape not only the minds but also the hearts of our students. By leading by example and embodying Stoic virtues in our interactions with students and colleagues, we can inspire a culture of resilience, wisdom, and compassion within our schools. Through reflection, dialogue, and intentional action, we embark on a journey of personal and professional growth, guided by the timeless wisdom of the Stoic sages.

As we conclude our exploration of Stoicism in education, let us state again our commitment to becoming more effective and enlightened teachers. May this book serve as a source of inspiration and guidance on our journey toward cultivating resilience, wisdom, and compassion in ourselves and our students. Let us continue to embrace the principles of Stoic philosophy and integrate them into our teaching practices, knowing that by doing so, we can make a profound difference in the lives of those we educate.

In closing, let us remember the words of Marcus Aurelius once more from *The Meditations*: "Waste no more time arguing about what a good man should be. Be one."(Aurelius, Book 10, section 16) As educators, let us strive to embody the virtues of Stoicism in our lives and in our classrooms, knowing that by doing so, we can truly make a positive impact on the world.

Alana Armstong

Supplementary Resources:

The following is a list of powerful Stoic quotes from the ancient Stoics organized by category:

Resilience:

"It's not what happens to you, but how you react to it that matters." Epictetus, a former slave turned Stoic philosopher, emphasized the power of perspective in shaping our response to adversity. As educators, we can draw strength from his teachings by reframing challenges as opportunities for growth and learning."
—Epictetus

"The impediment to action advances action. What stands in the way becomes the way."
—Marcus Aurelius

"Choose not to be harmed, and you won't feel harmed. Don't feel harmed, and you haven't been."
—Marcus Aurelius

"He who fears death will never do anything worthy of a living man." —**Seneca**

"Difficulties strengthen the mind, as labor does the body."
—**Seneca**

Integrity:

"Waste no more time arguing about what a good man should be. Be one."
—Marcus Aurelius

"It is better to live one day with honor, than a hundred years in disgrace."
— Seneca

"He is a wise man who does not grieve for the things which he has not, but rejoices for those which he has."
—Epictetus

"The soul's security lies in its strength, not in the luck of the world." **—Seneca**

Hope:

"The happiness of your life depends upon the quality of your thoughts."
—Marcus Aurelius

"While we wait for life, life passes."
—Seneca

"The only way to happiness is to cease worrying about things which are beyond the power or our will."
— Epictetus

"Never let the future disturb you. You will meet it, if you have to, with the same weapons of reason which today arm you against the present."
—Marcus Aurelius

Patience:

"No great thing is created suddenly."
—**Epictetus**

"The key is to keep company only with people who uplift you, whose presence calls forth your best."
—**Epictetus**

"He suffers more than necessary, who suffers before it is necessary." —**Seneca**

"If you are distressed by anything external, the pain is not due to the thing itself, but to your estimate of it; and this you have the power to revoke at any moment."
— **Marcus Aurelius**

Work Ethic:

"The best revenge is not to be like your enemy."
—Marcus Aurelius

"The soul's security lies in its strength, not in the luck of the world." **—Seneca**

"When you arise in the morning, think of what a precious privilege it is to be alive - to breathe, to think, to enjoy, to love."
—Marcus Aurelius

"Don't explain your philosophy. Embody it."
—Epictetus

Motivation:

"It is not death that a man should fear, but he should fear never beginning to live."
—Marcus Aurelius

"Wealth consists not in having great possessions, but in having few wants."
—Epictetus

"First say to yourself what you would be, and then do what you have to do."
—Epictetus

"You have power over your mind - not outside events. Realize this, and you will find strength."
—Marcus Aurelius

Kindness:

"Wherever there is a human being, there is an opportunity for kindness."
—Seneca

"Be kind, for everyone you meet is fighting a hard battle."
—Philo of Alexandria (Though not a Stoic, this quote is often associated with Stoic teachings)

"The best way to avenge yourself is to not become like the person who hurt you."
—Marcus Aurelius

"Treat your inferiors as you would be treated by your betters."
—Seneca

"If it is not right, do not do it; if it is not true, do not say it."
—Marcus Aurelius

"What progress, you ask, have I made? I have begun to be a friend to myself."
—**Seneca**

"No act of kindness, no matter how small, is ever wasted."
—**Aesop (not a Stoic philosopher, but aligned with Stoic values)**

"The happiness of your life depends upon the quality of your thoughts."
—**Marcus Aurelius**

"The highest good is to help others; the lowest is to hurt others."
—**Zeno of Citium**

"The greatest good you can do for another is not just share your riches, but reveal to them their own."
—**Seneca**

Hard Work:

"The harder you work, the harder it is to surrender."
—**Epictetus**

"No great thing is created suddenly, any more than a bunch of grapes or a fig. If you tell me that you desire a fig, I answer you that there must be time. Let it first blossom, then bear fruit, then ripen." —**Epictetus**

"The soul's security lies in its own strength, not in the luck of the world."
—**Seneca**

"Sweat equity is the most valuable equity there is. Know your business and industry better than anyone else in the world. Love what you do or don't do it."
—**Marcus Aurelius**

Acceptance:

"The first step to peace is to stand and accept."
—Epictetus

"He is a wise man who does not grieve for the things which he has not, but rejoices for those which he has."
—Epictetus

"Man is not worried by real problems so much as by his imagined anxieties about real problems."
—Epictetus

"There is only one way to happiness and that is to cease worrying about things which are beyond the power of our will."
—Epictetus

Virtue:

"What progress, you ask, have I made? I have begun to be a friend to myself."
—Seneca

"Virtue is the only good."
—Seneca

"The happiness of your life depends upon the quality of your thoughts."
—Marcus Aurelius

"To live a good life: We have the potential for it. If we can learn to be indifferent to what makes no difference."
—Marcus Aurelius

Stoic Quotes By Well Known People:

"The only way to deal with this life meaningfully is to find one's passion and put everything into it."
— **Nassim Nicholas Taleb**

"He who angers you conquers you."
— **Elizabeth Kenny**

"The things that we love tell us what we are."
—**Thomas Aquinas**

"Happiness is not something ready-made. It comes from your own actions."
— **Dalai Lama**

"To love and be loved is to feel the sun from both sides."
— **David Viscott**

"The only real prison is fear, and the only real freedom is freedom from fear."
— **Aung San Suu Kyi**

"Do not anticipate trouble, or worry about what may never happen. Keep in the sunlight."
— **Benjamin Franklin**

"You cannot control the behavior of others, but you can always choose how you respond to it."
— **Roy T. Bennett**

"Adopt the pace of nature: her secret is patience." — **Ralph Waldo Emerson**

"The greatest weapon against stress is our ability to choose one thought over another."
— **William James**

"Self-control is strength. Right thought is mastery. Calmness is power."
— **James Allen**

"The only limit to our realization of tomorrow is our doubts of today."
— **Franklin D. Roosevelt**

"Things that matter most must never be at the mercy of things that matter least."
— **Johann Wolfgang von Goethe**

"In the middle of difficulty lies opportunity."
— **Albert Einstein**

"Life is either a daring adventure or nothing at all."
— **Helen Keller**

"Life is 10% what happens to us and 90% how we react to it." — **Charles R. Swindoll**

"The mind is everything. What you think you become." — **Buddha**

"Success is not final, failure is not fatal: It is the courage to continue that counts."
— **Winston Churchill**

"The best way to predict your future is to create it."
— **Peter Drucker**

"In the end, we will remember not the words of our enemies, but the silence of our friends."
— **Martin Luther King Jr.**

"Your task is not to foresee the future, but to enable it." — **Antoine de Saint-Exupéry**

"Change your thoughts and you change your world."
— **Norman Vincent Peale**

"The only person you are destined to become is the person you decide to be."
— **Ralph Waldo Emerson**

"We must accept finite disappointment, but never lose infinite hope."
— **Martin Luther King Jr.**

"When we are no longer able to change a situation, we are challenged to change ourselves."
— **Victor Frankl**

"You have within you right now, everything you need to deal with whatever the world can throw at you."
— **Brian Tracy**

"Success is stumbling from failure to failure with no loss of enthusiasm."
— **Winston Churchill**

"It's not the years in your life that count. It's the life in your years."
— **Abraham Lincoln**

"Be not afraid of life. Believe that life is worth living, and your belief will help create the fact."
— **William James**

"You are never too old to set another goal or to dream a new dream."
— **C.S. Lewis**

"Act as if what you do makes a difference. It does."
— **William James**

"Believe you can and you're halfway there."
— **Theodore Roosevelt**

"Success is not how high you have climbed, but how you make a positive difference to the world."
— **Roy T. Bennett**

"The best way to find yourself is to lose yourself in the service of others."
— **Mahatma Gandhi**

"The mind is everything. What you think you become."
— **Buddha (his ideas have influenced modern philosophy)**

Educational Books which may be used in the Stoic Classroom:

Phil Van Treuren. *A Dog Who Follows Gladly*. Stoic Simple, 1 May 2023

---. *The Stoic Fable Book*. 25 Sept. 2023.

---. *The Stock Horse and the Stable Cat*. Stoic Simple, 1 Dec. 2021.

---. *The Little Book of Stoic Quotes*. Stoic Simple Press, 1 May 2024.

Holiday, Ryan, and Victor Juhasz. The Boy Who Would Be King. Ryan Holiday, 2020.

Mackesy, Charlie. Boy, the Mole, the Fox and the Horse. S.L., Ebury Press, 2019.

Breath and Visualisation Work for Personal Practice and Classroom Practice:

1. Basic Mindfulness Practice:

- Find a quiet and comfortable place to sit. Sit with your back straight and hands resting comfortably. Gently close your eyes or keep a soft gaze.
- Take a deep breath in through your nose, feeling your chest and abdomen expand. Exhale slowly through your mouth, feeling the release of tension. Let your whole body relax.
- Shift your focus to your breath. Notice the sensation of each inhale and exhale. Feel the cool air entering your nostrils and the warm air leaving. Take slow breaths.
- If your mind starts to wander, that's okay. Gently guide your attention back to your breath without judgment.
- Continue to breathe mindfully, fully present in each breath. If your thoughts drift, acknowledge them and return to the breath.
- After 5-10 minutes, slowly open your eyes, take a moment to reorient yourself, and carry the sense of mindfulness into your day.

2. Body Scan Mindfulness Exercise:

- Begin by finding a comfortable position, either sitting or lying down. Take a few deep breaths to relax.
- Focus your attention on your toes. Curl them tightly for a few seconds, then release. Feel the difference between tension and relaxation.
- Move to your feet, ankles, and gradually work your way up your body. Tense and then release each muscle group, paying attention to the sensations.
- As you scan, breathe naturally and notice any areas of tension or discomfort. Send your breath to these areas, allowing them to soften and relax.
- Continue the body scan, moving through legs, hips, torso, arms, and neck. Take your time and be present in each moment.
- Once you've reached the top of your head, take a few deep breaths, feeling the overall sense of relaxation throughout your body.

3. Loving-Kindness Mindfulness Session:

- Find a comfortable seat and close your eyes. Take a few moments to center yourself with a few deep breaths.
- Begin by bringing someone you love to mind, perhaps a close friend or family member. Picture their face and generate feelings of warmth and love.
- Silently repeat phrases like, "May you be happy, may you be healthy, may you be safe, may you be at ease." Feel the sincerity in each wish.
- Extend these wishes to yourself: "May I be happy, may I be healthy, may I be safe, may I be at ease." Embrace the positive intentions for your own well-being.
- Gradually extend these wishes to others in your life, and even to those you may find challenging. Allow the loving-kindness to radiate outward.
- Take a few moments to sit in the warmth of these feelings. When you're ready, open your eyes, carrying this sense of love into your interactions.

4. Beach Visualization:

- Get into a comfortable seated position, close your eyes, and take a few deep breaths to relax.
- Imagine yourself standing on a sandy beach. Feel the warmth of the sand beneath your feet.
- Hear the gentle waves as they rhythmically roll in and out. Listen to the seagulls in the distance.
- Picture the vast ocean stretching out before you. Notice the play of sunlight on the water.
- Engage your senses fully. Smell the salt in the air, feel the warmth of the sun on your skin, and taste the tang of the sea breeze. Feel the fresh air blowing against your face. The breeze gently blowing your hair.
- Stay in this visualization for a few more moments, absorbing the tranquility of the beach. When you're ready, open your eyes.

5. Forest Walk Visualization:

- Find a comfortable place to sit. Close your eyes, take a deep breath, and imagine yourself at the edge of a peaceful forest.
- Picture the entrance and start to walk slowly into the forest. Feel the crunch of leaves beneath your feet.
- Notice the tall trees surrounding you, their branches forming a canopy overhead. Listen to the rustling of leaves in the gentle breeze.
- Take in the scents of earth and pine. Take in the smell of the woods. Feel the cool shade and warmth of dappled sunlight on your skin.
- Continue walking deeper into the forest, exploring its beauty and serenity. Notice the golden light dancing in and out of the shadows of trees. Allow yourself to be fully present in this natural setting.
- When you're ready, open your eyes, bringing the tranquility of the forest with you.

6. Mountain Meditation:

- Sit comfortably with your back straight and close your eyes. Take a few deep breaths to center yourself.
- Visualize yourself at the base of a majestic mountain. Feel the solid ground beneath you.
- Start to ascend the mountain, feeling a sense of strength and purpose with each step.
- As you reach the summit, take in the expansive view. Recognize the challenges in your life as smaller in comparison.
- Connect with the stability and strength of the mountain. Breathe in deeply, absorbing this strength, and exhale any doubts or tension.
- When you're ready, open your eyes, carrying the metaphorical strength of the mountain into your day.

7. 4-7-8 Breathing Technique:

- Sit comfortably with your back straight. Close your eyes and take a few deep breaths to settle in.
- Inhale quietly through your nose for a count of 4. Feel your lungs expand fully.
- Hold your breath for a count of 7, allowing the breath to be retained gently.
- Exhale completely through your mouth for a count of 8, releasing any tension.
- Repeat this cycle for several breaths, allowing the rhythmic pattern to soothe your nervous system.
- When you're ready, open your eyes, feeling a sense of calm and centeredness.

8. Box Breathing:

- Find a quiet place to sit comfortably. Close your eyes and take a few deep breaths to settle in.
- Inhale slowly and steadily for a count of 4. Feel the breath filling your lungs.
- Hold your breath for a count of 4, experiencing the stillness and balance.
- Exhale smoothly for a count of 4, releasing any tension.
- Pause for another count of 4, allowing a moment of quiet before the next breath.
- Continue this rhythmic breathing, feeling a sense of balance and relaxation with each cycle.
- When you're ready, open your eyes, carrying this centeredness into your day.

9. Body-Mind Relaxation:

- Find a quiet and comfortable place to sit or lie down. Close your eyes and take a few deep breaths to relax.
- Begin by focusing on your toes. Curl them tightly for a few seconds, then release completely.
- Move to your feet, arches, and heels. Tense these muscles and then let go, allowing a wave of relaxation to wash over your feet.
- Continue this process, moving through each muscle group in your legs, hips, abdomen, chest, back, arms, and neck.
- As you release tension, visualize any stress or tightness melting away. Feel a sense of lightness and ease spreading throughout
 your body.
- When you've completed the sequence, take a few moments to enjoy the overall sensation of relaxation. When you're ready, open your eyes.

10. Warmth and Comfort:

- Find a quiet and comfortable place to sit or lie down. Close your eyes and take a few deep breaths.
- Imagine a warm, comforting light surrounding your body. Visualize this light as a soft, golden glow.
- As you inhale, imagine this light entering your body and spreading warmth to every muscle, starting from your toes and moving upward.
- With each exhale, visualize tension and stress leaving your body as dark clouds dissolving into the air.
- Continue to breathe deeply, allowing the comforting light to envelop you. Feel a deep sense of relaxation and security.
- When you're ready, open your eyes, carrying this warmth and comfort with you.

11. Letting Go of Stress:

- Find a quiet and comfortable place to sit. Close your eyes and take a few deep breaths to settle into the present moment.
- Begin by acknowledging any sources of stress in your life. Picture each one without judgment.
- As you exhale, visualize these sources of stress turning into clouds. With each breath out, see these clouds dissipating into the air.
- Feel a sense of lightness and release with each exhale. Allow the weight of stress to lift, leaving you with a calm and peaceful mind.
- Take a few more moments to breathe and enjoy the sensation of letting go. When you're ready, open your eyes, carrying this sense of calm into your day.

12. Stream of Thoughts Meditation:

- Find a comfortable place to sit. Close your eyes and take a few deep breaths to center yourself.
- As you sit, observe your thoughts without judgment. Imagine each thought as a leaf floating down a gentle stream.
- Watch these thoughts drift by without holding onto any. If a thought lingers, acknowledge it and let it continue downstream.
- Feel the stream carrying away any stressful or negative thoughts, leaving your mind clear and calm.
- Enjoy the quiet space between thoughts. When you're ready, open your eyes, carrying this sense of mental clarity into your day.

13. Gratitude Reflection:

- Find a comfortable place to sit. Close your eyes and take a few deep breaths to center yourself.
- Think of three things you're grateful for today. Visualize each one in detail, immersing yourself in the sights, sounds, and emotions.
- Feel a sense of warmth and appreciation in your heart. Allow these feelings to expand as you express gratitude for each aspect of your life.
- Take a few more moments to bask in the positive energy of gratitude. When you're ready, open your eyes, carrying this appreciation with you.

Whether you're using it for meditation, manifestation, or a simple gratitude journal, you can see a lot of movement in emotional blockages by incorporating it into your daily routine.

14. Positive Affirmations:

- Find a quiet and comfortable place to sit. Close your eyes and take a few deep breaths to settle in.
- Repeat positive affirmations silently or aloud. Choose affirmations that resonate with you, such as "I am calm and centered" or "I choose peace over stress."
- Visualize these affirmations becoming a reality in your life. Picture yourself embodying the qualities expressed in each affirmation.
- Feel the positive energy flowing through you with each repetition. Take a few moments to enjoy the sense of empowerment and positivity.
- When you're ready, open your eyes, carrying this positive mindset into your day.

15. Body Scan for Sleep:

- Find a comfortable position in bed, lying on your back. Close your eyes and take a few deep breaths to relax.
- Begin a gentle body scan, starting with your toes. Feel the weight of your toes sinking into the bed as you release any tension.
- Move to your feet, ankles, and slowly scan up through your legs, hips, and torso. Release tension with each breath.
- Continue to scan through your arms, neck, and head. Imagine each body part becoming heavy and relaxed.
- Visualize a soft, soothing light enveloping your entire body. Feel the warmth of this light promoting a sense of calm and tranquility.
- As you drift into sleep, allow the comforting sensations to guide you to a restful night. Sweet dreams.

Works Cited:

Aurelius, Marcus, and Gregory Hays. Meditations. New York, Modern Library, 6 May 2003.

Epictetus. The Manual for Living. Strelbytskyy Multimedia Publishing, 8 Jan. 2021.

Epictetus, and Hastings Crossley. The Golden Sayings of Epictetus with the Hymn of Cleathes. Translated and Arranged by Hastings Crossley, Etc. London, Macmillan & Co.; Macmillan Co, 1903.

Seneca. Seneca's Letters from a Stoic. David & Charles, 2016.

Lucius Annaeus Seneca, and Edward Phillips Barker. Letters to Lucilius. Oxford, Clarendon Press, 1932.

Rizvic, Sejla. "Teachers, Facing Increasing Levels of Stress, Are Burned Out." The New York Times, 13 Mar. 2023, www.nytimes.com/2023/03/13/education/teachers-quitting-burnout.html.

Roy, Sandip. "Find Peace without Religion: A Non-Religious Serenity Prayer." The Happiness Blog, 26 Dec. 2022, happyproject.in/non-religious-serenity-prayer/. Accessed 20 Aug. 2024.

Phil Van Treuren. The Little Book of Stoic Quotes. Stoic Simple Press, 1 May 2024.

- - -. "Stoic Simple Press." Stoic Simple, https://www.stoicsimple.com/stoicism-books/.

Flourishafter. "15 Free Guided Meditation Scripts for Relaxation - Flourishafter40."
Flourishafter40, 11 Nov. 2023, flourishafter40.com/15-free-guided-meditation-scripts/#1-basic-mindfulness-meditation.